# Feeling Good About Others
## Activities to Encourage Positive Interaction

by
Debbie Pincus

illustrated by Judy Hierstein

Cover by Judy Hierstein

Copyright © 1994, Good Apple

ISBN No. 0-86653-794-5

Printing No. 987654321

**Good Apple**
**1204 Buchanan St., Box 299**
**Carthage, IL 62321-0299**

*Paramount Publishing*

MALONE·BROWN

# Dedication

To the memory of my dad, Dr. William Pincus, and to my close friends, Mark Lasky and Laura Pem-Bourget.

# Acknowledgement

To my husband, Richard Ward, and to my two beautiful children, Jake and Derek–a family committed to getting along together. Also, thanks to my nieces and nephews, Scott and Lindsay Eisberg and Katherine and Lawson Ballard. They continue to show me what getting along together is all about. Thanks to Camille Farrow for typing this manuscript.

GA1488

# Table of Contents

GA1488

# Introduction

Getting along with others requires empathy, trust, respect, assertion, good self-esteem, tolerance, acceptance and compromise, to name a few attributes. It also takes the development of communication skills. These attributes and skills must be learned.

*Feeling Good About Others* is an activity book designed to help young people develop these building blocks to getting along with others. It offers students a fun, action approach to learning the ingredients of and enhancing the skills of interacting effectively and becoming successful in interpersonal relationships.

## Note to Teachers

The book is divided into ten chapters. Each chapter is about one of the building blocks of the pyramid to feeling good about others. Each chapter includes a vocabulary page called Word Buster. The new vocabulary words should be discussed before doing any of the activities on the pages that follow. The fuzzy monster described on each Word Buster page can be found on one of the pages in the book. The clue at the bottom of each Word Buster page will help the student locate the fuzzy monster. The fuzzy monster has eyes and looks furry.

An activity should not be started by students until a class discussion of the topic takes place and directions are given. An activity should not be completed until a class discussion takes place and a connection is made between the building block (for example, trust or empathy) and getting along with others.

## Note to Students

Each activity is intended to enhance your abilities to get along with others. The better able you are to get along with others, the better you will feel about yourself and those around you. Have fun with each activity and ask your family to try the activities with you. They may want to join in the fun and learn more about you and themselves.

## Note to Family

Your child will best learn to get along well with others by learning the skills of interpersonal relations. Take time each day to listen and take an interest in what your child is learning by participating in the activities. Discuss your child's feelings and your own. Share your difficulties and successes in your own interpersonal relations. The more you relate to and show interest in your child, the better the two of you will get along.

GA1488

# Chapter 1

**Building Blocks to Getting Along**

# Word Buster 1

There is a fuzzy monster who tries to mess up other children's games, good times, and friendships. Can you capture it? It is on the loose. As you complete each chapter's Word Buster, you will get another clue. Put all the clues together in order to capture the fuzzy monster.

Look up the meaning of each word below, and write its definition. Then write a story that includes at least five of the words. Your story should introduce us to the antics of the fuzzy monster who does not know how to get along with others.

## Words          Definitions

recipe: _____

trust: _____

assertive: _____

etiquette: _____

empathy: _____

compromise:_____

communication: _____

respect: _____

selfish: _____

hate: _____

fear: _____

antic:_____

pyramid: _____

quality: _____

ingredient: _____

Write your story on the next page. The fuzzy monster clue will be on the bottom of the next page.

# Buster Story

Write a story about the fuzzy monster who does not know how to get along with others. Be sure to illustrate your story and use at least five words from Word Buster 1 on page 2.

_____

_____

_____

_____

_____

_____

_____

_____

_____

_____

_____

_____

_____

_____

_____

_____

Read your story to your teacher and classmates.

**Fuzzy Monster Clue 1:**

The fuzzy monster is hidden somewhere in this book.

# Building Blocks

What are the building blocks to getting along with others? Cut out those blocks below and paste them in the boxes on page 5.

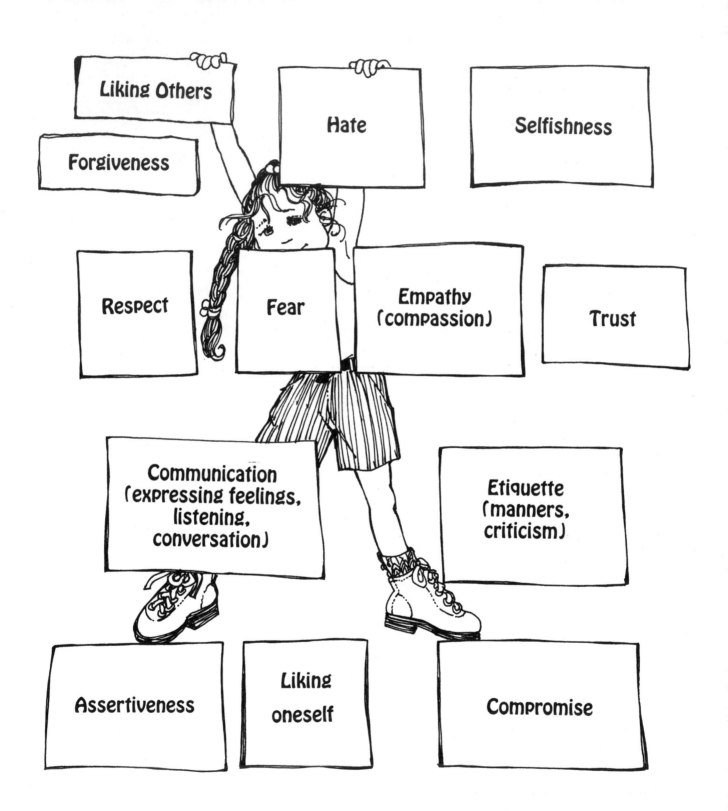

# Pyramid

Build a pyramid of blocks that shows the skills of getting along with others. Cut the blocks out from page 4 and paste in the correct boxes below. Each chapter will teach you one of these skills.

# Give Examples

Give examples of the following and then discuss them with your teacher and classmates. Show times that you've exhibited some of these behaviors.

Give three examples of *trusting* behavior.

1. _____

2. _____

3. _____

Give three examples of *empathetic* behavior.

1. _____

2. _____

3. _____

Give three examples of *respectful* behavior.

1. _____

2. _____

3. _____

Give three examples of *good communication* between two people.

1. _____

2. _____

3. _____

Give three examples of *assertive* behavior.

1. _____

2. _____

3. _____

GA1488

# Climbing the Ladder

Put an *X* on each rung of the ladder after you give an example of how you've shown or expressed each of the following behaviors with your friends, classmates, or family members.

Example: I sent a thank-you note after I stayed at my friend's house.

Discuss with your teacher or classmates what these behaviors have to do with getting along with others. How does using these behaviors help you to be liked by others and to like yourself?

# Recipe for Getting Along

Make a recipe that would describe the ingredients of getting along with others. Think of a person with whom you get along well. What are the qualities you both share which help you get along together? List them below. Examples: care, love, generosity.

### Qualities You Both Share

Now write them as a recipe and give the recipe to this person. (The recipe on the left is an example, and the list on the right shows some words which may be useful in writing another recipe of your own.)

## Use recipe words like:

mix
dash
stir
add
tsp.
tbsp.
sauté

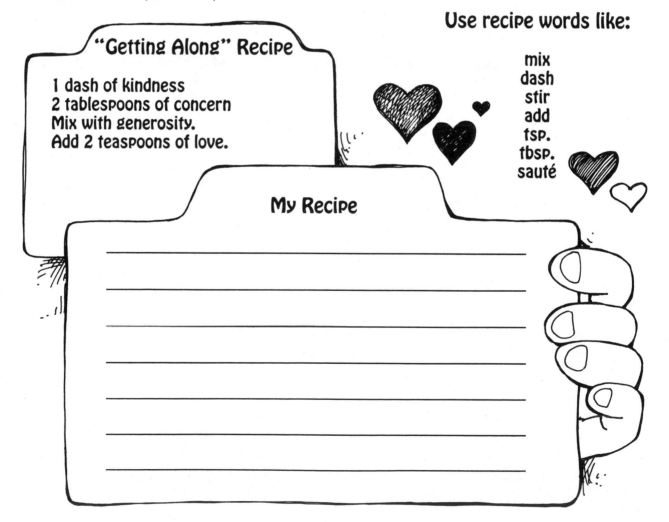

### "Getting Along" Recipe

1 dash of kindness
2 tablespoons of concern
Mix with generosity.
Add 2 teaspoons of love.

### My Recipe

8

GA1488

# Bouquet of Roses

Each day try to express each of the behaviors below to those with whom you interact. Every time you do exhibit a behavior, pick that flower by cutting it out and pasting it on the flower stems to make a bouquet. Hopefully by the end of each day you will have a bouquet of roses for yourself or to give to someone you care about.

(Make several copies of this page so you can have one for every day.)

GA1488

# Chapter 2
# Building Trust

10

# Word Buster 2

Circle the words below in red when you find them on one of the pages in the "Building Trust" chapter. Copy the sentence in which you find it below and guess the word's meaning. Then look up each word's meaning and write the dictionary definition in the space provided.

**Interaction** (sentence) _____

_____

(guess meaning) _____

_____

(dictionary definition) _____

_____

**Sequence** (sentence) _____

_____

(guess meaning) _____

_____

(dictionary definition) _____

_____

**Fuzzy Monster Clue 2:**
The fuzzy monster is female.

GA1488

# Trust Means . . .

Find the definition of *trust* in your dictionary. Write it below.

_____

_____

_____

_____

_____

Draw or cut out a picture that would illustrate the meaning of *trust*. Hang it on your classroom bulletin board.

What do you think trust has to do with getting along with others?

_____

_____

_____

_____

_____

_____

GA1488

# Show Me I Can Trust You

Imagine you are Kathy. Which interaction would help you develop trust with Matthew? Discuss your reasons with your teacher and classmates.

| **Earlier** | **Later** |
|---|---|

**A.** I'll call you so we can make plans for tomorrow.

I guess Matthew changed his mind about our plans for today. He never called.

**B.** I promise I won't tell anyone what you told me.

Wait until I tell you what Kathy told me. But you have to promise not to tell her I told you.

**C.** I feel bad, Matthew, because my brother is not nice to me.

Sounds like you are really sad about it.

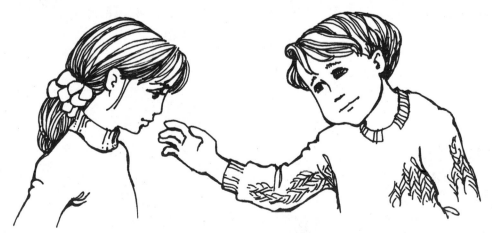

What does trust have to do with getting along with others?

13

# Flying High with Trust

Draw a line from the word *trust* to anything that helps develop it. Color in the balloon and strings when you finish.

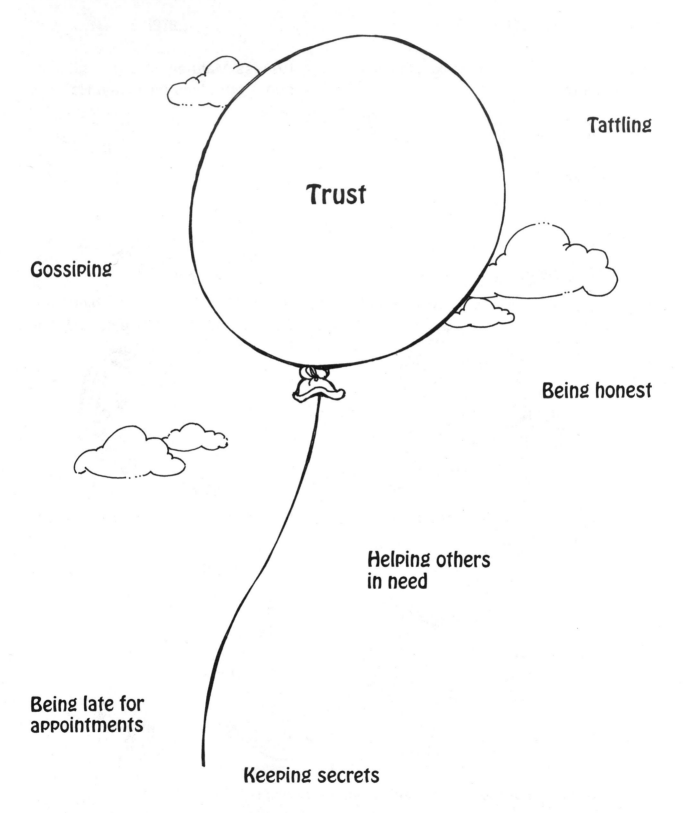

Tattling

Trust

Gossiping

Being honest

Helping others
in need

Being late for
appointments

Keeping secrets

Discuss with your teacher and classmates why these behaviors help develop trust between people. What does trust have to do with getting along with others?

14

GA1488

# A Trusting Ending

Complete this story so that Molly and Jake end up trusting each other. Read your story to your teacher and classmates.

Jake was very angry with Molly. Molly had promised him that she would trade him some baseball cards and then decided to keep them for herself. _____

_____

_____

_____

_____

_____

_____

_____

_____

_____

_____

_____

_____

_____

_____

_____

**Ending**

Jake and Molly came to really trust each other.

What does trust have to do with getting along with others?

GA1488

# I Trust You

Name a person you would trust to help you with your homework. How has this person shown trust to you? _____

_____

Name a person you would trust to listen if you had a problem. How has this person shown trust to you? _____

_____

Name a person you would trust to help you fix a broken toy. How has this person shown trust to you? _____

_____

Name a person you would trust to be by your side if you were sick. How has this person shown trust to you? _____

_____

Name a person you would trust to tell your deepest secret to. How has this person shown trust to you? _____

_____

Look over what you have written.

Can you trust more than one person? _____

Can you trust different people for different things?_____

What do you think people trust the most about you? Why? _____

_____

How have you proven to them you could be trusted? _____

_____

Write a note to each of the people you have listed and tell each why you trust him or her. _____

_____

What does trust have to do with getting along with others? _____

_____

GA1488

# To Trust or Not to Trust

A woman who is a stranger to Melissa walks up to her on the playground. The woman says to Melissa, "Hi, my name is Sara. I'm a friend of your mother's. She asked me to pick you up from school today. My car is right here." Melissa likes people, gets along well with them, and has learned they can be trusted. She goes with the woman.

Do you think Melissa made a good decision? Why or why not? _____

_____

_____

What would you have done and why? _____

_____

_____

Could she have done something differently before going with this woman? What? _____

_____

_____

Do you believe you should always trust someone right away? Why or why not? _____

_____

_____

Should you trust anyone in order to get along with him or her? Explain. _____

_____

_____

Discuss the questions and your answers with your teachers and classmates.

# Building of Trust

Cut out the boxes and paste them in a sequence that shows the building of trust between two people. Paste your sequence below. Discuss with your teacher and classmates the behaviors that build trust. What does trust have to do with getting along with others?

Dustin tells Justin that he's a good friend and they go and play together.

Recess is about to begin and Dustin hopes to find some kids to play with.

The softball game gang tells Justin that they don't care if he leaves the team.

The softball players tell Dustin to get lost.

Justin walks off the field and runs over to Dustin.

Dustin's friend, Justin, tells the softball gang with whom he's playing that they can get lost if that's the way they treat his friend, Dustin.

Dustin wants to be included in the softball game that's already begun.

GA1488

# Chapter 3

# Learning to Like Oneself

# Word Buster 3

As you read through chapter 3, identify any words whose meanings you do not know. Write each of these words below. Look up the meaning of each word in the dictionary and write it next to the word.

_____

_____

_____

_____

_____

_____

_____

_____

_____

_____

_____

_____

_____

_____

_____

**Fuzzy Monster Clue 3:**

The fuzzy monster is hidden in one of the activity pages, and she is very round.

GA1488

# Treasure Chest

Hunt through this chest and find those qualities that you most treasure about yourself. Color them your favorite color. Fill in your other qualities in the empty boxes.

**My name is** _____.

Cut out your treasure chest and hang it on the bulletin board. See if your classmates can guess which chest is yours by looking at the qualities that you have colored. Discuss with your teacher and classmates what treasuring yourself has to do with getting along with others.

GA1488

# Liking Your Actions

What actions do you think will help Jake like himself? Put an X in those boxes. Discuss your reasons with your classmates and teacher.

Jake says "thank you" for a gift his uncle bought him even though Jake did not like the gift.

Jake apologized to his sister after hurting her feelings.

Jake told a white lie to his friend because he didn't want to hurt his feelings.

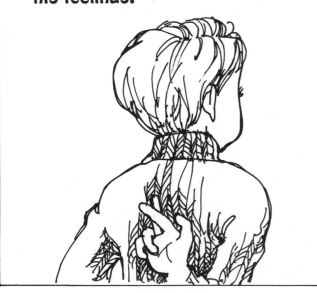

Jake never returned a toy he had borrowed from a friend.

What does behaving in ways that you feel good about have to do with liking yourself?

22

GA1488

# Mosaic

The mosaic below contains ten boxes. In three of the mosaic boxes, write three actions (one in each box) that helped you to like yourself. Color those boxes green.

Write three actions in the mosaic (one in each box) that caused you not to feel good about yourself. Color these boxes orange.

Write two actions in the mosaic (one in each box) that caused others to respect you. Color those boxes red.

Write two actions in the mosaic (one in each box) that caused you to *trust* yourself. Color those boxes yellow.

Share with your teacher and classmates. Discuss what respecting, liking, and trusting yourself have to do with getting along with others.

GA1488

# All About Liking Myself

If I like myself, then others will probably like me because _____

_____

_____

_____

_____

_____

If I like myself, then I will probably like other people because _____

_____

_____

_____

_____

_____

If I were a friend of mine, the things I would like about me would be _____

_____

_____

_____

_____

Discuss your answers with your teacher and classmates.

# Wanted

Make a wanted poster of yourself. Hang it on your classroom bulletin board.

## WANTED

Put your photo here.

_____ is
(your name)

wanted by many people for _____

_____

(Write qualities about yourself that

_____

cause people to want to be with you.)

_____

_____ is wearing
(your name)

_____

_____ and is

(Describe yourself physically.)

_____ and can often be found doing

(Write the activities you spend time doing.)

_____

# Plain Jane Question

Answer this question and explain: Why should Jane like herself if she is not the prettiest, smartest, or most popular student?

_____

_____

_____

_____

_____

Are these good reasons to like yourself? _____

Do you feel you have to be the *best* or *most* in order to like yourself? Explain.

_____

_____

_____

Does anyone make you feel unloved if you are not the best or the most?

_____

How do you feel about this? _____

Do you like people only if they are the best or most? What are other reasons to like yourself?

_____

GA1488

Chapter 4

Learning to
Like Others

GA1488

# Word Buster 4

Unscramble each word and look up its definition. Write its meaning next to the unscrambled word.

**e e r n g t y o s i** _____

_____

_____

**u l i a q y t** _____

_____

_____

**m o u a c l f g e a** _____

_____

_____

**r e a e t l o t** _____

_____

_____

**a t s o b** _____

_____

_____

## Word Bank

tolerate        camouflage
generosity     quality
boast

**Fuzzy Monster Clue 4:**

The fuzzy monster is camouflaged on one page of this book.

# Apple Tree

Pick the apples which describe the qualities you look for in a friend. Color them red. Add your own to the blank apples.

Understanding

Talker

Boaster

Generosity

Kindness

Ability to Share

Selfishness

Honesty

Discuss with your teacher and classmates what the qualities you have chosen have to do with getting along with others.

GA1488

# Liking to Like

Decide what you find likable about each person described below. Write your response on the lines below each box.

┌─────────────────────────────────────┐
│ A boy who helps to cheer up a        │
│ sick friend although the sick        │
│ friend doesn't want cheering         │
└─────────────────────────────────────┘

_____

_____

┌─────────────────────────────────────┐
│ A girl who gets scolded by her       │
│ father for helping a stranger to     │
│ his car after her father told her    │
│ not to talk to strangers             │
└─────────────────────────────────────┘

┌─────────────────────────────────────┐
│ A boy who hugs all of his            │
│ friends but forgets to introduce     │
│ them to one another                  │
└─────────────────────────────────────┘

_____        _____

_____        _____

_____        _____

Can you find something likable in people even if they do unlikable things? Explain.

_____

_____

_____

What is important about finding what is likable in others? What does that have to do with getting along with others?

_____

_____

_____

30

GA1488

# Sneaky Jealousy

Write the dictionary definition of *jealousy* below.

_____

Write five things that make you jealous of others.

1. _____

2. _____

3. _____

4. _____

5. _____

How do you treat others when you feel jealous of them?

_____

Has anyone ever been jealous of you? How did he or she treat you? How did it make you feel?

_____

Do you think the emotion of jealousy causes you not to like someone else even though he or she has done nothing wrong?

_____

How does jealousy get in the way of getting along with others?

_____

Discuss with your teacher and classmates some ways to get over your jealous feelings and ways to prevent these feelings from occurring.

_____

Of whom are you jealous in your class? Can you discuss your feelings with that person?

_____

Make a booklet. On each page write something that causes you to feel jealous of another person. Illustrate each page.

GA1488

# Likable Figures

Write a different friend's name under each figure. Then write five likable qualities about each person. Share your feelings with each of those friends.

# A Portrait of a Friend

Laura can be described as extremely sensitive. If criticized, she will attack. She can be loud when she feels she is not getting enough attention and selfish when you ask her for help. She will tattle on you if you don't act the way she thinks you should.

There's a difference between *liking* someone's behavior and *accepting* that behavior. You may not like that your friend is loud, but you may be able to accept that your friend needs to be loud. You understand this person's need for attention. Therefore, although you don't like your friend's behavior, you can accept, expect, and tolerate it.

If Laura was your friend, list which of her behaviors you would *dislike but could accept* and which you would *dislike but could not accept*. Discuss your response with your teacher and classmates.

| Dislike but Could Accept | Dislike but Could Not Accept |
| --- | --- |
| _____ | _____ |
| _____ | _____ |
| _____ | _____ |
| _____ | _____ |
| _____ | _____ |
| _____ | _____ |
| _____ | _____ |
| _____ | _____ |

What does accepting someone's behavior have to do with getting along?

GA1488

# The Beginning

Write the beginning and middle to this story after reading the ending. Hang your story on the bulletin board.

_____

_____

_____

_____

_____

_____

_____

_____

_____

_____

_____

_____

_____

_____

_____

_____

**Ending**

Derek had always disliked his younger brother, Matthew. After all that had happened, he learned to like him, even love him, and now they get along well!

Chapter 5

Developing Empathy

# Word Buster 5

Look up the meaning of each word below and write its definition next to it. Then see if you can find the words in the word search below.

gossip: _____

tattle: _____

successful: _____

emotion: _____

response: _____

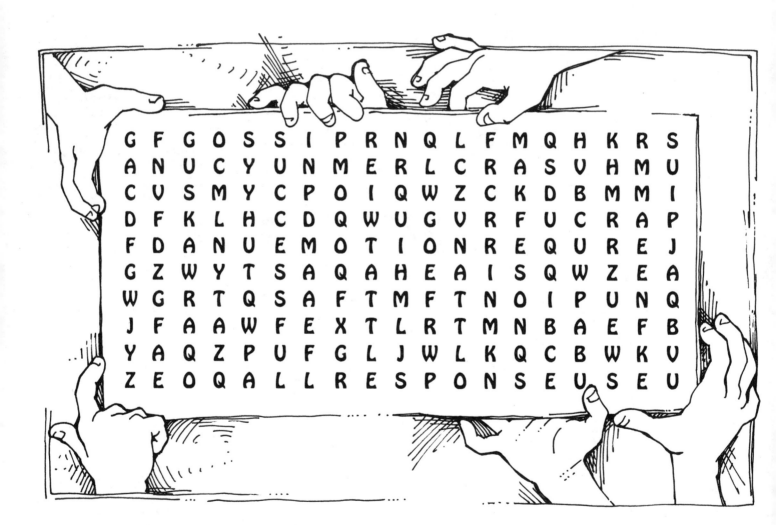

```
G  F  G  O  S  S  I  P  R  N  Q  L  F  M  Q  H  K  R  S
A  N  U  C  Y  U  N  M  E  R  L  C  R  A  S  V  H  M  U
C  V  S  M  Y  C  P  O  I  Q  W  Z  C  K  D  B  M  M  I
D  F  K  L  H  C  D  Q  W  U  G  V  R  F  U  C  R  A  P
F  D  A  N  U  E  M  O  T  I  O  N  R  E  Q  U  R  E  J
G  Z  W  Y  T  S  A  Q  A  H  E  A  I  S  Q  W  Z  E  A
W  G  R  T  Q  S  A  F  T  M  F  T  N  O  I  P  U  N  Q
J  F  A  A  W  F  E  X  T  L  R  T  M  N  B  A  E  F  B
Y  A  Q  Z  P  U  F  G  L  J  W  L  K  Q  C  B  W  K  V
Z  E  O  Q  A  L  L  R  E  S  P  O  N  S  E  U  S  E  U
```

**Fuzzy Monster Clue 5:**
The fuzzy monster knows how to put an end to things.

36

GA1488

# Empathy

Find a dictionary definition of *empathy* and write its meaning below.

_____

_____

_____

Describe a situation in which you felt *empathy* for someone else.

_____

_____

_____

Describe a situation in which someone else was *empathetic* with you. How did it make you feel?

_____

_____

_____

What do you think developing *empathy* for other people has to do with getting along with them?

_____

_____

_____

GA1488

# Empathetic Tic-Tac-Toe

Put an *X* in the boxes that show Kathy's empathy towards Jill. See if you can get tic-tac-toe.

| Jill does not get chosen to act in the class play. | | Jill is cold and mean to her friend, Kathy, who does get chosen. |
|---|---|---|
| Kathy remembers a time she felt jealous of someone and acted meanly to that person. This helps her understand Jill. | Kathy tells Jill that she understands that under her meanness she's very upset. | Kathy gossips to all her friends about Jill. |
| Kathy says to Jill, "I'm sorry you did not get the part in the play. If you feel like talking or crying, I'm here to listen." | Kathy says to Jill, "You'd better stop acting mean to me or I'll tell on you." | Kathy acts cold and mean to Jill. |
| Kathy asks Jill to stop being mean to her and also tells her that she knows she must feel hurt and jealous. She would feel the same way. | Kathy ignores Jill and leaves her out of her new group of friends, all of whom have been selected to be in the class play. | Kathy tells Jill that she never wants to be friends with her again. |

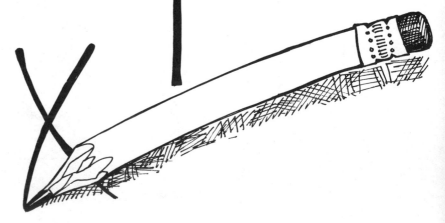

# Why?

Why do you think Jack is doing what he is doing?

| Jack is getting little attention at home from his parents. | Jack is at school pushing and shoving his way in line. | The teacher yells at him after his classmates tattle. |
|---|---|---|

Why do you think Jack pushes when he is standing in line? Does it have anything to do with how he feels his parents treat him? Explain.

_____

_____

Is he successful at getting what he wants? Explain. Have you ever felt like Jack? Have you ever behaved the way he did?

_____

_____

By understanding why Jack does what he does, are you more able to like him?

_____

_____

What would be a good way of getting along with Jack? What does Jack need from people? Discuss with your teacher and classmates.

_____

_____

Why is understanding our friends' behavior rather than judging behavior more helpful in getting along with them?

_____

_____

GA1488

# How Would You Feel If . . . ?

Imagine you are Sara. How would you feel if you were in her shoes? Cut out a cartoon face that would show your emotion in each situation and paste in the appropriate box.

| The other children laugh at Sara.  | Paste a picture of how you would feel here. |
| --- | --- |
| Sara is the only child to fail the math test.  | Paste a picture of how you would feel here. |
| Sara finds a cat and her parents allow her to keep it.  | Paste a picture of how you would feel here. |

Why is it important to imagine how you would feel in someone else's shoes in order to develop empathy? Discuss with your teacher and classmates.

_____

_____

_____

_____

_____

GA1488

# Imagining

Why might these people be feeling the way they are feeling? Choose one character and write a story below about how that person has come to feel the way he or she does. Share your story with your teacher and classmates.

**Justine**

**Cary**

**Jared**

**Naomi**

## Write On!

Why does this character feel this way? How would you feel if you were this person? Have you ever felt this way? What caused you to feel that way? What would this character need in order to feel differently? What would you need?

_____

_____

_____

_____

_____

_____

_____

_____

_____

_____

GA1488

# Getting into His Shoes

You cut in front of Sammy in the lunch line. How would you feel if you were in Sammy's shoes? Draw yourself in his shoes and describe your emotion.

You do not let Jared play with you, and then you tell all your friends at recess. How would you feel if you were in Jared's shoes? Draw yourself in his shoes and describe your emotion.

Discuss with your teacher and classmates what getting in someone else's shoes has to do with getting along with others.

_____

_____

_____

_____

_____

GA1488

# Responding Empathetically

An empathetic response helps another person feel understood and cared about. Which responses do you think would be empathetic ones? Circle them below.

I feel so upset about the test results.

Big deal.

You deserve to fail.

You feel very badly about your grade.

I see that you are feeling sad.

Who cares?

I understand how you feel. I would feel the same way if I were you.

Study harder next time.

Discuss with your teacher and classmates what empathetic responses are, how they make others feel, and why they are important in getting along with others.

_____

_____

_____

_____

_____

_____

_____

_____

GA1488

# On Your Mark, Get Set, Go

At the count of three make a list of all the empathetic responses you can think of for the statement below. Read them aloud to your classmates and list them all on a large sheet of paper.

> **My parents are always fighting, and I get sick of hearing their arguments.**

## Empathetic Responses

_____

_____

_____

_____

_____

_____

_____

_____

_____

_____

_____

_____

_____

_____

_____

_____

# Empathy Bingo

Every time you respond in one of the ways listed below, put an *X* in the box. If you get five *X*s in a straight line (horizontally, vertically, or diagonally), you have bingo and lots of empathy! Try to get bingo once a day. Make copies of this page so you can play it daily.

B I N G O

| | | | | |
|---|---|---|---|---|
| Thank someone for his or her thoughtful action. | Help someone with a difficult task without complaining. | Respect the opinion of someone with whom you disagree. | FREE | Give a hug to a person who needs it. |
| Tell someone that you understand (if you do). | Ask someone who feels left out to join in (secretly). | Listen to someone. | Help someone who is in need of help. | FREE |
| Tell someone that you will be a shoulder for him or her to cry on, if he or she should need to cry. | Imagine how someone feels and reflect it back to him or her. Say, "Sounds like you are feeling _____." | FREE | Understand someone's behavior rather than judge the person. Tell him or her you understand. | Tell someone he or she can trust you. Show how trustworthy you are. |
| FREE | Look someone in the eye when he or she is speaking to you; show how well you listen. | Share with someone who is sad a time when you had a similar feeling, so he or she knows he or she is not alone. | Help someone feel special if he or she is not feeling special. | Find something of value about a person with whom you don't get along. |
| Hold the hand of someone who needs a hand to hold. | FREE | Be with someone who is feeling lonely. | Listen with open ears and an open heart to someone. | Tell someone you care and show him or her how caring you are. |

45

# Chapter 6

# Building Respect for Others

GA1488

# Word Buster 6

Look up the meaning of each word below and write its definition next to it. Then scramble each word and ask a classmate to unscramble the words.

regard: _____

describe: _____

complain: _____

hinder: _____

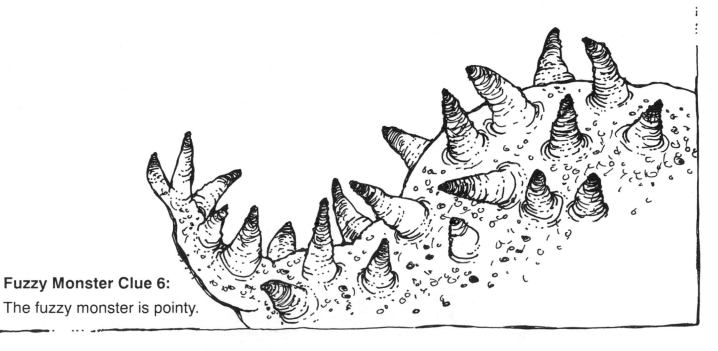

**Fuzzy Monster Clue 6:**

The fuzzy monster is pointy.

GA1488

# Defining Respect

You as a class member should write your definition of *respect*—what it means to you. Write your definition on a slip of paper and hand it in (without your name) to your teacher. Your teacher will write on a slip of paper the dictionary definition of *respect*. The teacher will then read aloud every definition. Each person should guess which is the dictionary definition. Compile *all definitions* and hang them on your bulletin board after the discussion.

_____

_____

_____

_____

_____

_____

_____

_____

_____

_____

_____

_____

_____

_____

_____

_____

# Respect

Use each letter of *respect* and write a word or sentence that helps define *respecting others*. The first one has been done for you.

**R**   Regard for others' feelings helps you to get along with others.

**E**  _____

**S**  _____

**P**  _____

**E**  _____

**C**  _____

**T**  _____

GA1488

# Write On

Write a story that describes how Anne grew to respect Marisa and how her respect helped them to get along. Put your stories together in a class book called *Respect*. Remember to illustrate your story.

_____

_____

_____

_____

_____

_____

_____

_____

_____

_____

_____

_____

_____

_____

_____

_____

_____

_____

GA1488

# Once upon a Time . . .

Describe a time when you acted respectfully to someone. How did you feel? How do you think the other person felt? How did treating someone respectfully help you to get along together?

_____

_____

_____

_____

_____

_____

_____

# RESPECT

Describe a time when someone acted respectfully towards you. How do you think the other person felt? How did being treated respectfully help you to get along better?

_____

_____

_____

_____

_____

_____

_____

51

GA1488

# Finding Respect

What is respectful about each person's behavior? Describe the respectful behavior underneath each picture.

| A child asks an elderly man if he needs help carrying his groceries. | A child invites another child who is alone to join in her game. | A child shares her toys. |
| --- | --- | --- |

# Cut and Paste

What are the building blocks to becoming a person who is respected by others? Cut those blocks out and paste them below. Discuss the blocks you have not cut out with your teacher and classmates. Why do these blocks hinder your ability to be respected? Discuss the blocks you have cut out and discuss why you chose them.

| Complaining about things without working toward changing things | Not talking behind other people's backs |
|---|---|
| Taking for yourself without considering the other person | Teasing others |
| Sharing with others even when you might want what you have for yourself | Helping create change when possible and necessary |
| Treating others with respect | Finding a way to bring happiness and joy to yourself and others |

GA1488

# Can You . . . ?

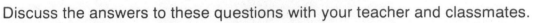

Discuss the answers to these questions with your teacher and classmates.

1. Can you ever respect a person who sometimes hurts your feelings? Explain.

_____

_____

_____

2. Can you ever respect a person who is *always* mean to other people and to animals? Explain.

_____

_____

_____

_____

3. Can you ever respect a person you don't like? Explain.

_____

_____

_____

_____

4. Can you ever respect a person who is not smart or good looking? Explain.

_____

_____

_____

54

GA1488

# Chapter 7

# Building Communication

# Word Buster 7

Write down any word you come across in the chapter for which you do not know the meaning. Write its definition below.

| Words | Definitions |
|---|---|
|  |  |
|  |  |
|  |  |
|  |  |
|  |  |
|  |  |
|  |  |
|  |  |
|  |  |
|  |  |
|  |  |
|  |  |
|  |  |
|  |  |
|  |  |
|  |  |
|  |  |

**Fuzzy Monster Clue 7:**

The fuzzy monster always comes through in the end.

GA1488

# What Is Good Communication?

As we discuss what *good communication* means, we will use the word "effectively." What does *effectively* mean? Look up *effectively* in the dictionary and write its meanings on the line below. Good communication means listening and responding *effectively* to one another.

Effectively: _____

Example:

Listening and responding effectively means hearing what the other person is saying and responding in a way that will help you to be heard.

List as many phrases as you can think of to complete each sentence below.

Good listeners that I've known are good listeners because . . .

- _____
- _____
- _____
- _____
- _____
- _____
- _____

Good responses that I've heard are good responses because . . .

- _____
- _____
- _____
- _____
- _____
- _____
- _____

GA1488

# Good Communication

Color the scene below which describes "good" communication between two people. Then discuss with your teacher and classmates how the scene displays good communication.

1.

GA1488

# How Would You Feel If . . . ?

Pretend you are Trevor. How would you feel if someone was speaking to you the way Henry is speaking to him? In scene A? In scene B? Draw in Henry's face describing how you might feel if you were Henry in each scene.

What does good communication have to do with others' feelings?

_____

What does good communication have to do with good feelings about yourself and others?

_____

Can you describe a situation in which the way you were spoken to helped you feel good about yourself? The way you spoke to someone else?

_____

GA1488

# Keys to Good Communication

Color the keys your favorite colors. Which are the keys to good listening?

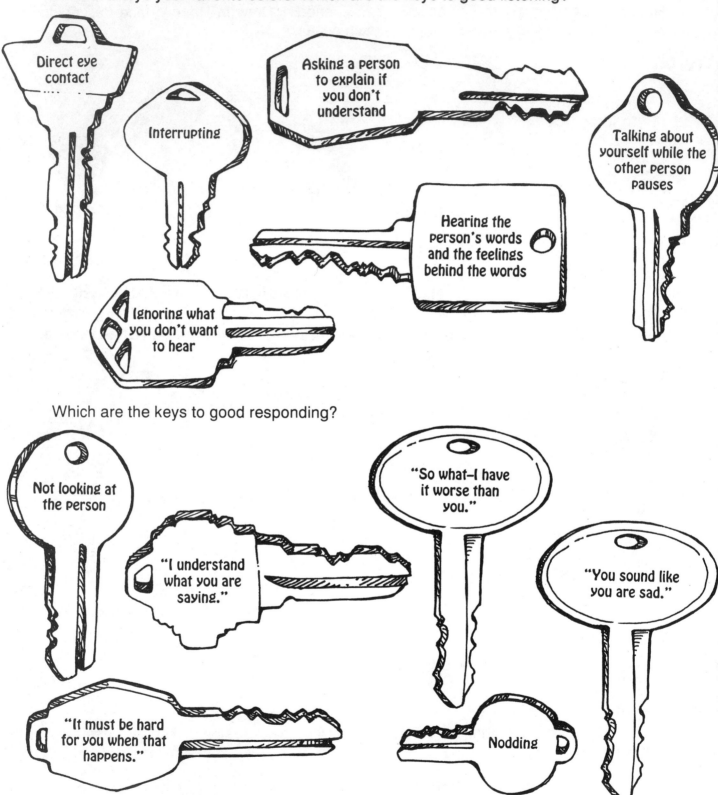

Direct eye contact

Interrupting

Asking a person to explain if you don't understand

Talking about yourself while the other person pauses

Hearing the person's words and the feelings behind the words

Ignoring what you don't want to hear

Which are the keys to good responding?

Not looking at the person

"I understand what you are saying."

"So what—I have it worse than you."

"You sound like you are sad."

"It must be hard for you when that happens."

Nodding

Discuss with your teacher and classmates the reasons behind your choices.

Continue by turning to page 61.

GA1488

# The Door to Open Communication

Cut out the keys to good communication on page 60. Paste one key on each door below. Display this page in your classroom, school, or home to remind others of the keys to good communication.

# Doors of Opportunities

What doors get opened for you if you are a good communicator? Draw a red circle around those doors.

GA1488

# Skills to Good Communication

Hanah is angry with Zoe for pushing her while they are standing in line.

What went wrong with Hanah's and Zoe's communication?

_____

_____

Why do you think Zoe responded to Hanah in such a mean way?

_____

_____

Do you think Hanah could have communicated to Zoe in a way which would have helped Hanah to be heard and respected? What would you suggest?

_____

_____

When a person feels attacked by another person (blamed, called names, etc.), the other person usually defends himself or herself by attacking back rather than really listening and communicating effectively. It seems like Zoe felt attacked by Hanah and attacked Hanah back. Both people probably ended up feeling hurt and misunderstood or angry and distrusting.

If Hanah told Zoe what she felt when being pushed in line instead of calling her names, Zoe might have understood her feelings. This would be an example of *effective* communication. For example, Hanah might have said, "I *felt upset* that you pushed me while we were standing in line. Next time please tell me if you are angry about something and maybe I can do something about it."

Examples of feeling words:

| | | | |
|---|---|---|---|
| sad | angry | happy | frustrated |
| upset | hurt | disappointed | excited |

63

GA1488

# Zoe's Response

Part of effective communication is responding to the other person in a way which communicates empathy and understanding. Imagine that Hanah communicates her feelings effectively to Zoe.
For example:

> I felt upset that you pushed me in line, Zoe. Please be careful next time.

Zoe is not being blamed or attacked. Hanah is simply explaining her feelings. Since Zoe is not under attack, she will not be so defensive, and she is free to hear what Hanah is saying and to understand her feelings.

Effective responses would include Zoe listening carefully to Hanah's feelings and reflecting back to Hanah what she's heard.

> You feel upset that I pushed you in line yesterday.

Then Zoe could again respond with understanding.

> I'm glad you understand. It makes me feel better.

> I'm sorry for making you feel bad. I understand that my pushing you would be upsetting.

> I will try to be more careful next time.

64

GA1488

# Me, Me, Me

List as many endings as you can for each sentence.

I'm a good listener because I . . .

- _____
- _____
- _____
- _____
- _____

I'm a good responder because I . . .

- _____
- _____
- _____
- _____
- _____

I could improve my listening skills by . . .

- _____
- _____
- _____
- _____

I could improve my responding skills by . . .

- _____
- _____
- _____
- _____

GA1488

Chapter 8

Learning to
Be Assertive

66

# Word Buster 8

Write each word's meaning and then use all the words in a short story entitled "My Friend Next Door."

deny:_____

enable: _____

bully: _____

firm: _____

respect:_____

rude: _____

ruthless: _____

appropriate: _____

formula: _____

manipulate: _____

_____

_____

_____

_____

_____

_____

_____

**Fuzzy Monster Clue 8:**

The fuzzy monster is last but not least.

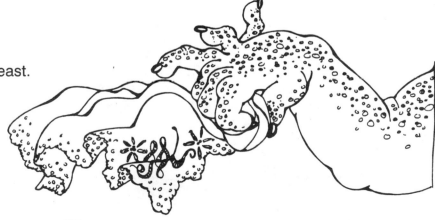

GA1488

# What Is Assertiveness?

*Assertive behavior* is defined as "enabling a person to act in his or her own best interests, to stand up for herself or himself without undue anxiety, to express honest feelings comfortably, or to exercise personal rights without denying the rights of others."

Answer the following questions and then discuss this with your teacher and classmates:

Do you think behaving assertively helps a person to get along with others? Why or why not? Explain.

_____

_____

_____

_____

_____

_____

_____

Describe a time when acting assertively helped you get along better with some-one.

_____

_____

_____

_____

_____

_____

_____

GA1488

# Aggressive or Assertive?

*Aggressive behavior* is defined as "accomplishing a goal at the expense of others." Aggressive behavior hurts other people in the process by making trouble for them or manipulating them.

Remember, *assertive behavior* is defined as "enabling a person to act in his or her own best interest, to stand up for himself or herself and to experience feelings comfortably without denying the rights of others."

Read the following scenarios and color the pieces of the window red if the behavior is aggressive, and color the pieces your favorite color (other than red) if the behavior is assertive.

Discuss the differences with your classmates and teacher.

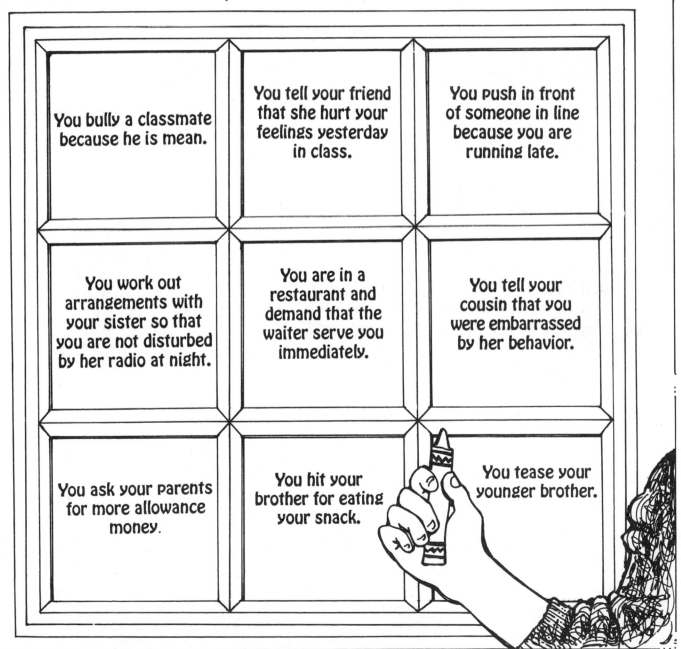

You bully a classmate because he is mean.

You tell your friend that she hurt your feelings yesterday in class.

You push in front of someone in line because you are running late.

You work out arrangements with your sister so that you are not disturbed by her radio at night.

You are in a restaurant and demand that the waiter serve you immediately.

You tell your cousin that you were embarrassed by her behavior.

You ask your parents for more allowance money.

You hit your brother for eating your snack.

You tease your younger brother.

GA1488

# How Would You Feel If . . . ?

How would you feel if your brother demanded that you help him immediately?

_____

_____

How would you feel if your classmates pushed in front of you in line?

_____

_____

How would you feel if you were bullied by your friend?

_____

_____

How would you feel if your sister was honest with you about her feelings?

_____

_____

How would you feel if your brother worked out a plan with you so you could both watch what you wanted on TV?

_____

_____

In which behavior, assertive or aggressive, do you end up feeling respected? In which do you end up feeling hurt? Disrespected?

_____

_____

Which behavior helps you to get along better with others? To feel good about yourself and others? Why?

_____

_____

GA1488

# What Are Assertive Behaviors?

Circle in green the assertive behaviors listed below. Write one in each of the window boxes.

honest

firm

pushy

loud

respectful

hurtful

direct

responsible

rude

ruthless

appropriate

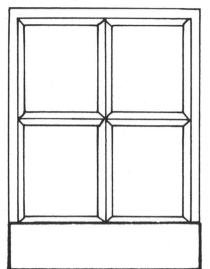

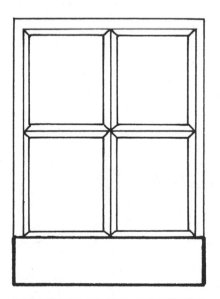

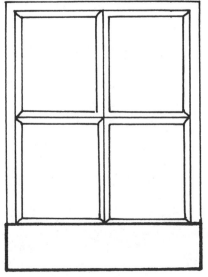

GA1488

# Right On!

Circle in orange the boxes with which you agree. Discuss your reasoning with your teacher and classmates.

GA1488

# What Would You Do If . . . ?

Complete each "what if" with an assertive way of behavior.

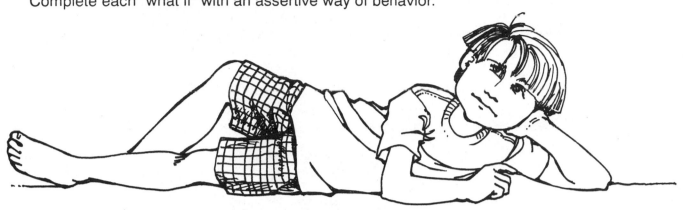

What would you say if you were in a restaurant and someone behind you was blowing smoke from a cigarette at you?

_____

_____

_____

What would you say if you were at a party but did not know anyone but the host? You want to get to know people.

_____

_____

_____

What if you were in the grocery store and someone cut in front of you in line?

_____

_____

_____

What would you say if your friends were not including you in their conversation?

_____

_____

_____

GA1488

# Whose Problem Is It?

Read the situation below.

Draw an X over the situation in which you think it would be appropriate to be assertive. Explain your reasons with your teacher and classmates.

Remember: If another person's behavior affects you, then it is appropriate to be assertive. If his or her behavior has little effect on your life, then you may be overstepping your bounds to be assertive.

Wearing a new blue dress

GA1488

# The Assertive Formula

When responding assertively, use the formula below. Begin with "when you" and describe the behavior you have a problem with followed by "I feel" and a feeling word. Then say "I would like/want/need" and finally express what you seek. For example: Your friend always says she'll come over to your house and always cancels. You might say:

*When you* plan to come to my house and always cancel, *I feel* disappointed. *I would like* you to stick to what you say.

Try filling in the others:

* Your brother always rides your bike.

    When you _____, I feel _____. I would like

    _____.

* Your friend copies your homework.

    When you _____, I feel _____. I would like

    _____.

Write some other assertive statements that you could use in your own life. Try using them the next time one of these problems comes up.

_____

_____

_____

_____

_____

GA1488

# Chapter 9

Learning to Compromise

# Word Buster 9

On the lines below write any words from chapter 9 for which you do not know the meanings. Find their definitions.

| Words | Definitions |
|-------|-------------|
|       |             |
|       |             |
|       |             |
|       |             |
|       |             |
|       |             |
|       |             |
|       |             |
|       |             |
|       |             |
|       |             |
|       |             |
|       |             |
|       |             |
|       |             |
|       |             |

**Fuzzy Monster Clue 9:**

The fuzzy monster puts a stop to things.

GA1488

# On Your Mark, Get Set, Go!

Write the definition of *compromise*.

_____

_____

_____

Now write several examples of compromises you've made with others. You have four minutes. On your mark, get set, go!

_____

_____

_____

_____

_____

_____

Read your examples aloud to your teacher and classmates. Discuss how it feels to make compromises, how it helps you to get along with others, and why compromises are necessary.

_____

_____

_____

_____

_____

# Working Out a Compromise

A compromise usually involves two or more people who have conflicting wants or needs. Example: Jason wants his brother to turn the light out after 8:00 p.m. so he can go to sleep. His brother Luke needs to do his homework after 8:00 p.m. because he gets home from soccer practice late.

So the brothers decide to work out a compromise. These are the steps they take.

**Step 1**

They write out their two conflicting needs.

Jason wants the lights out by 8:00 p.m.
Luke needs the lights on after 8:00 p.m.

**Step 2**

They brainstorm all possible solutions.

Jason and his brother come up with any ideas (as crazy as they may sound) that would solve their problem. They write down any ideas that are said. They do not judge or discount any idea, no matter how crazy it is. (This process helps creativity.)
a. Luke would do his work in another room.
b. Jason would wear a blindfold to bed.
c. Luke would do his homework in the dark.

**Step 3**

Now they read each possible solution that has been brainstormed. They cross out any ideas that wouldn't work for either person.

a. Luke would do his work in another room.
b. ~~Jason would wear a blindfold to bed.~~
c. ~~Luke would do his homework in the dark.~~

They decide to cross **b** out because Jason did not want to sleep with a blindfold on, and he also felt he would still have to deal with the noise that Luke would make while doing his homework.

They decided to cross **c** out because Luke said it would be impossible to work in the dark.

They agreed on **a** and felt that would be the best compromise. Jason could sleep and Luke could get his work done anytime he needed.

Try using these steps to work out a compromise with a friend or relative. Discuss your process with your teacher or classmates.

GA1488

# Compromise Solution

Ian wants to play ball with his father on Sunday, but his father wants him to finish his book report that is due Monday. Work out a compromise solution for them.

_____

_____

_____

_____

Gary wants to watch the ball game with his brother, but his brother wants to watch it alone with his friends. Work out a compromise solution for them.

_____

_____

_____

_____

You want to sit in the front seat of the car whenever you ride with the family. Your sister also wants the front seat. What compromise are you willing to make with your sister so the two of you get along?

_____

_____

_____

_____

Discuss with your teacher and classmates why you think it is important to compromise. What does it have to do with getting along?

_____

_____

_____

_____

GA1488

# Sharing Sisters

Color the boxes red that describe compromises to the situation below. Color the boxes yellow that describe people being unreasonable.

## Situation

On Sunday morning you want to play with some new toys alone.

Your sister wants to play with them by herself.

Your father says you must work out a way to get along and not fight over the toys.

You scream at her and make her feel guilty.

You and your sister decide that you will play with them for fifteen minutes, and then she will play with them for fifteen minutes.

You throw up your hands in disgust and go do something else.

You and your sister decide to play with them together.

Discuss with your teacher and classmates what all compromises have in common. What does compromising have to do with getting along?

_____

_____

_____

_____

_____

_____

_____

GA1488

# Computerized Compromise

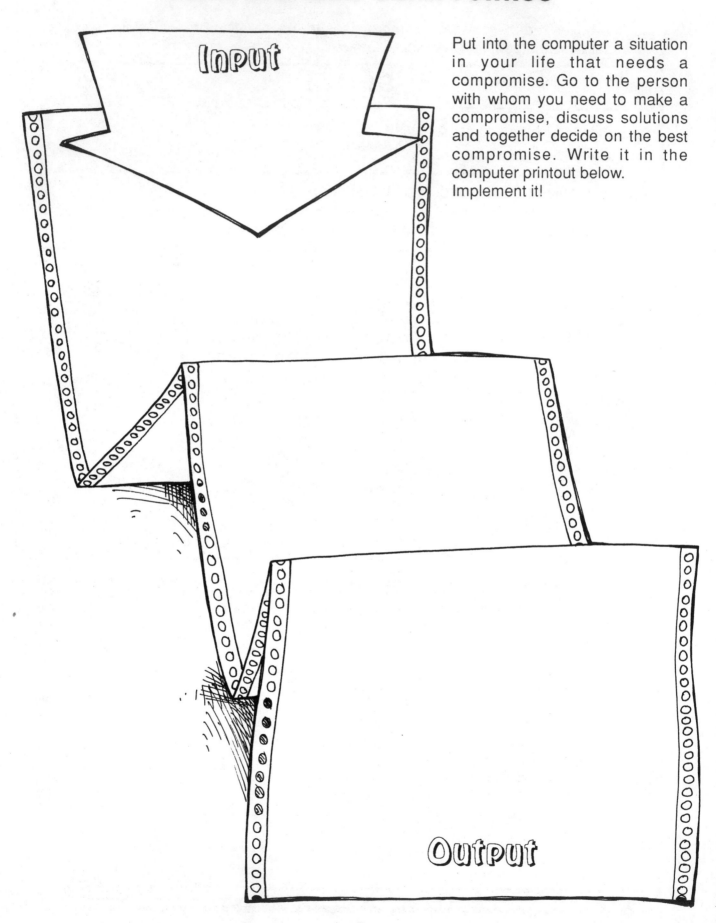

**Input**

Put into the computer a situation in your life that needs a compromise. Go to the person with whom you need to make a compromise, discuss solutions and together decide on the best compromise. Write it in the computer printout below.
Implement it!

**Output**

82

GA1488

Chapter 10

Building
Etiquette
Skills

83

# Word Buster 10

Unscramble the following words and find their definitions. The word bank may be helpful in finding the words. Write below.

edniifet        _____        _____

sdipopatni      _____        _____

tussaicitneh    _____        _____

pohmc           _____        _____

### Word Bank

chomp
definite
enthusiastic
disappoint
fantastic
reasonable

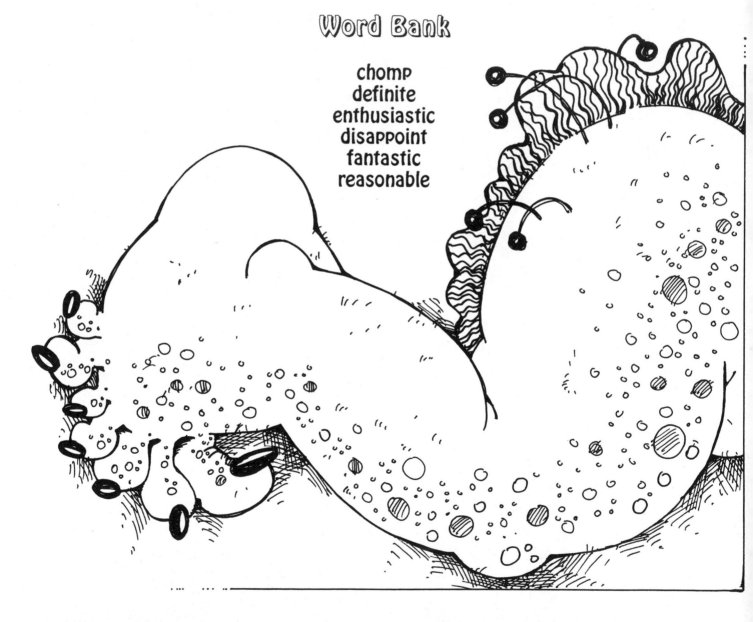

**Fuzzy Monster Clue 10:**

The fuzzy monster is close by.

84

GA1488

# Why Etiquette?

What is etiquette? Write the definition below.

_____

_____

_____

List as many reasons as you can think of for using etiquette with others. Combine your list with your classmates and make a big list for your bulletin board.

_____      _____

_____      _____

_____      _____

_____      _____

_____      _____

_____      _____

_____      _____

_____      _____

_____      _____

_____      _____

_____      _____

Discuss with your classmates and teacher what etiquette has to do with getting along with others.

The fuzzy monster is the period at the end of this sentence ✿

GA1488

# Colorful Etiquette

Use your favorite color to color the boxes that show good etiquette. Then discuss with your teacher and classmates why using this behavior would help you to get along with others.

| | | |
|---|---|---|
| **You do not RSVP\* for a party since you are not planning to go.**  | **You offer your friends some juice and snacks if they are at your home.** 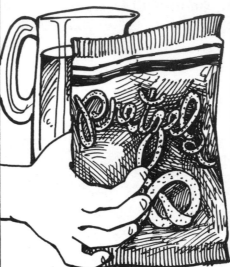 | **You ask others if they want any more food after you take the last bite.**  |
| **When your friends arrive, you take their coats and hang them up.**  | **You win all the prizes at your own birthday party.**  | **You take ice cream from the freezer without asking your brother if he would like some.**  |

\* Ask your teacher what *RSVP* means if you do not know.

GA1488

# Telephone Etiquette

Imagine you are speaking on the other end of this telephone. Write words in the word balloons that would show good etiquette.

Discuss telephone etiquette with your teacher and classmates. Why is it important in getting along with others?

87

# Table Manners

Write a behavior on each napkin that would describe good table etiquette. Write on each plate a behavior that would describe poor table etiquette.

**Eating with your mouth open.**        **Keeping elbows off the table.**

**Chomping your food.**        **Speaking with your mouth full.**

**Putting your napkin on your lap.**        **Eating the last bite before asking if others want any.**

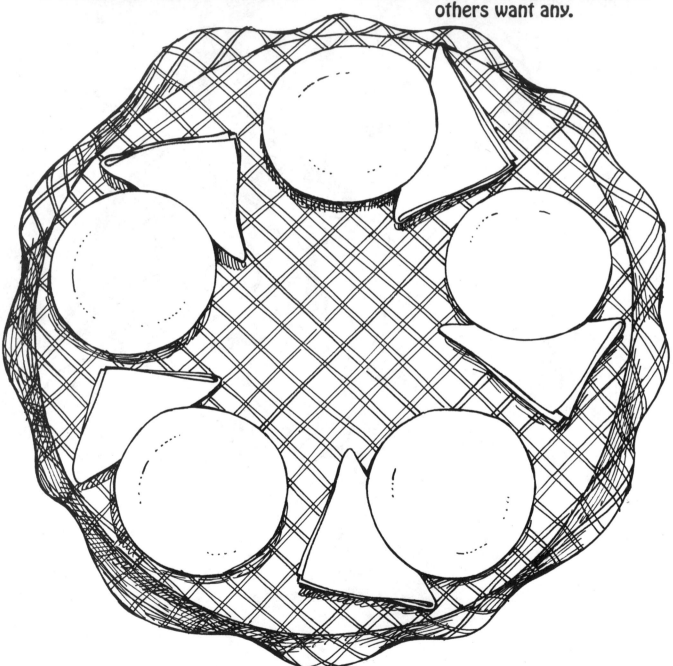

Discuss with your teachers and classmates what good table etiquette has to do with getting along with others.

GA1488

# Party Etiquette

Read the following story. Circle in red any behavior that Olivia exhibits which displays poor etiquette. Discuss your reasons with your teacher and classmates.

## The Party

Olivia received a party invitation from Laura, a classmate. Olivia got very excited. She jumped up and down enthusiastically and told all her other classmates that she got invited to Laura's party. She told Laura that she would definitely come to the party. Olivia bought Laura a present on her way home from school. When Olivia got home and told her parents about the party, her parents reminded her that the day of the party was during the week they'd be away on vacation. She would not be able to attend. Olivia was very disappointed and cried. Her mother comforted her. Olivia decided that the only good thing about not going to the party was that she could keep the present for herself. Olivia decided that there was no need to tell Laura that she would not be able to attend the party. Laura would probably not know the difference since so many other kids would be there.

## Questions to Discuss

1. Should Olivia have told all her classmates of her invitation? Why or why not?

2. Should Olivia have told Laura that she would attend the party before she checked with her parents? Why or why not?

3. Should Olivia keep the present for herself or give Laura a gift even though she will not be attending? Why or why not?

4. Should Olivia RSVP and tell Laura that she will not be attending her party? Why or why not?

Rewrite this story with Olivia exhibiting proper party etiquette.

# Etiquette Recipe

What are the ingredients for good etiquette? Create your recipe below.

**Use recipe words like:**

mix
dash
beat
stir

**Example of an etiquette recipe:**

1 dash of *empathy*
Mix with a cup of *thoughtfulness.*
Add *respect.*

Put all of the recipes into a class recipe book. Make a copy of the book for everyone. Make a new recipe a day to share with your friends. What does etiquette have to do with feeling good about your friends?

# Fuzzy Monster

Did you find the fuzzy monster? _____

Where was it hiding? _____

On what page? _____

Cut it out and paste it behind the prison bars below.

Remind the fuzzy monster of five important ingredients in getting along with others.

GA1488

# Reflections and Changes

Think about your answers to the following questions. Discuss these with your teacher, classmates, and the important people in your life.

• Who are the people you would like to get along with better?

• What has been difficult about getting along with each of these people?

• Which of your behaviors and attitudes need to change in order to get along better with these people?

• Are you willing to make these changes?

Take action—start now! See how your own feelings about yourself and others become more positive as you initiate change.

GA1488